8D Problem Solving Process

Martha Begley Schade

8D Problem Solving Process

Copyright © 2013 Martha Begley Schade

All rights reserved.

Table of Contents

Preamble 3

Guidelines on 8D Problem-Solving 7

Step D0: Preparing and Planning 13

Step D1: Form Your Team 15

Step D2: Describe the Problem 19

Step D3: Planning Containment Actions 25

Step D4: Determine the Root Cause 30

Step D5: Choosing & Verifying Corrective Actions 34

Step D6: Set Corrective Measures 38

Step D7: Take Preventive Measures 42

Step 8: Congratulate Your Team 47

8D Report Template 53

About the Author 56

Copyright & Disclaimer

The author and publisher have made every effort to produce a high quality, informative and helpful document. However, they make no representation or warranties of any kind with regard to the completeness or accuracy of the contents of the document. They accept no liability of any kind for any losses or damages caused or alleged to be caused, directly or indirectly, from using the information contained in this document. The information presented herein represents the view of the author as of the date of publication. Because of the rate at which conditions change, the author reserves the right to alter and update her opinion based on the new conditions. The report is for informational purposes only.

While every care has been taken in the compilation of the information, no responsibility of any nature whatsoever shall be accepted for any inaccuracies, errors or omissions. The information provided should not be treated as a substitute for advice. While every care has been taken in the compilation of the support resources attachment, no responsibility of any nature whatsoever shall be accepted for any inaccuracies, errors or omissions, or for the accuracy of any information contained in the attachment.

This report is not intended for use as a source of legal or accounting advice. You should be aware of any laws which govern business transactions or other business practices in your country and state.

Any reference to any person or business whether living or dead is purely coincidental.

Copyright © 2013 by Martha Begley Schade.

All rights reserved worldwide.

Preamble

The aim of this eBook is to give you a process by which you can carry out the 8D Process within your organization in the most efficient manner possible.

It aims to provide beginners to the 8D Process with a set of guidelines of what is expected during each step of the process.

It will make this process understandable and useful for every person, regardless of their academic background. It will support people who work in the handling of claims, in internal problem solving or in improvement programs.

It can also function as a master template for company internal training as well as a reminder for any veteran of the requirements for each step.

To supplement this eBook, we have a specific page for 8D Resources. Check this page regularly for updates.

History of 8D

Contrary to common belief, the 8D methodology originated in the U.S. Department of Defense (DOD) in 1974 and was called: "MIL-STD 1520 Corrective Action and Disposition System for Nonconforming Material". While this standard was officially abolished in 1995, the 8D methodology was driven by Ford in the automotive industry and is well known worldwide as a method of dealing with customer complaints effectively.

Benefits of adopting the 8D Approach

- Helps develop rapid response to customers and strengthens your relationship with them.

- Helps improve quality and saves money through less waste.

- Supports prevention rather than detection of problems.

- Reduces variations and improves the efficiency of your company's processes.

- Increases company internal knowledge and supports lateral improvements of other processes.

- Opportunity for innovation and innovative problem solutions.

The Implications of doing an 8D report

Your reputation and relationship with the customer will increase very positively. Depending on how well your response is as a company to this customer's complaint, you are dealing with the risk of losing that customer to your competitor.

The knock-on effect of doing a bad job of dealing with the customer complaint properly is loss of good will and good reputation. This will have implications on any potential customers and new business.

There may be legal implications, depending on the costs incurred from delivering defective parts. The insurances covering your company on such issues may require seeing effective action being taken to support continuation of their policies.

Remember too that the approach you take to dealing with this customers complaint will also be viewed during any upcoming Audits by external groups; certifying agencies, customers, financial auditors.

When done well, the new knowledge gained from the work done will increase the in-house expertise. The knowledge gained can be replicated in other processes, leading to all round quality improvements and a reduction of cost-intensive waste.

Reading Processes

In the case that you are not familiar with processes, here is a description of the symbols used in the diagrams:

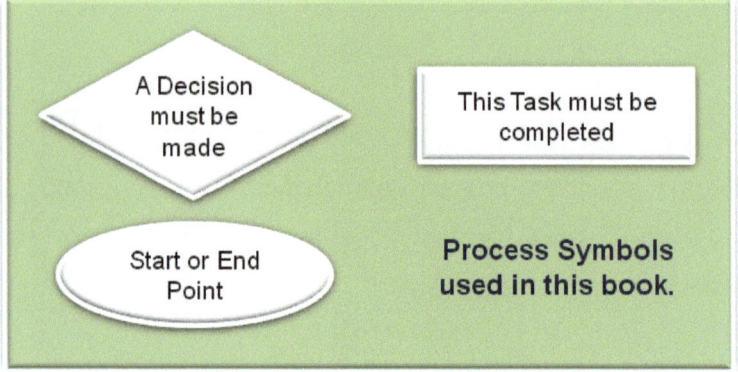

Guidelines on 8D Problem-Solving

The 8D problem-solving method, also known as the 8D plan, describes a process of steps to be taken in order to solve a customer complaint problem methodically.

The benefit of the method is the complete and thorough approach which enables us to solve current issues and improve problematic situations in a company immensely.

Depending on the nature of the problem, a team or an individual can work through these steps in order to discover the improvement possible.

Importance of an 8D Report

The 8D report serves as a checklist as well as a means of tracking improvement measures decided upon. Due to its importance, please consider delegating the role of document manager to a member of the team. This checklist helps to ensure that all steps are completed.

The 8D report is a part of the 8D problem-solving methodology and at the end of each step, is brought up to date. Any documents completed as a result of actions taken then become part of the report.

Therefore the report mirrors the current status of the problem-solving work and is to be seen as a "living *document*".

Consider using a **project notebook** to keep all documentation filed together in.

- The completed documentation can be stored as a valuable source of knowledge for the future. With many lessons to be learned from them, they can help solve other problems that may occur later on.
- Important Aspects to be taken into consideration: The aim of the 8D problem-solving process is to increase the likelihood of effectively solving problems in the production and R&D functions and to increase customer satisfaction.
- Remember too that in some countries, the authorities may need to sign off on the planning as they will need to accept the outcome of the report.

The Steps of 8D

The Steps in 8D are:

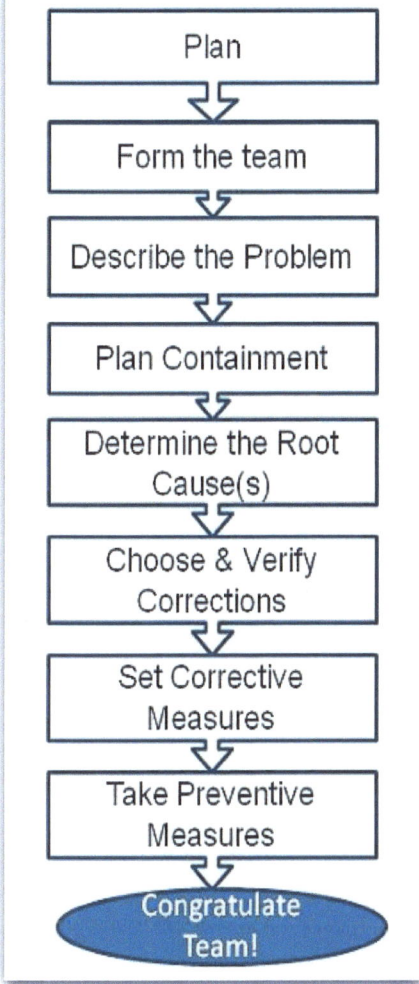

D0 Planning the project

D1 Forming your team of experts

D2 Describing the problem

D3 Acting immediately for damage limitation.

D4 Analyzing and determining the root cause(s) of the problem

D5 Choosing corrective actions and then verifying them.

D6 Setting the corrective actions

D7 Preventing recurrence

D8 Congratulating your team on a job well done.

The Rules of doing 8D

The following is important for the successful completion of the 8D problem-solving process:

1. **Ensure mandate from top management:** Make sure you get the mandate from top management as top management decisions and backing are very likely to be needed during the process.

2. **Enlist managerial support** by frequently informing them of developments within the process. Be prepared for the pressure from management as they are also under pressure from the customer. This pressure exerted can often lead to a rushed job and a failed problem-solving process. Have a named champion in management, someone who will champion your needs through, especially when more resources are needed, i.e. financial supports.

3. **Choose the right team:** Ensure that those people with the best knowledge of the processes or topic in question are involved. The team constellation may change over time working on the process, so it is important to have a core team of people with direct and clear responsibilities. Have someone responsible for ensuring the gathering of information, someone responsible for sharing the information while others may have the responsibility of

doing tests. Continuously evaluate the needs, capabilities and responsibilities of the team with each step.

4. **Formulate an accurate description of the problem:** They say that the better you describe a problem, the closer you are to the solution. Use questions such as: What is the problem? / What is it not? Where is the problem? / Where is it not? How widespread is the problem? / How far does it not go to (any limits recognizable)?

5. **Avoid skipping through steps:** Often, due to time constraints, there is an urge to skip through steps. This must always be avoided.

6. **Ensure co-operation within the team:** Remembering the stages of teamwork of Forming, Norming, Storming and Performing and the typical effects each stage has, ensure that all members of the team cooperate fully. Remember too, people often don't know how much they know until they actually start exchanging with others.

7. **Maintain Momentum:** Often there is the danger that the team members converge to such a degree that they fail to set priorities or fail to have a systematic approach in carrying out the analyses. So, keep that momentum going by setting your goals and following them.

8. **Understand the difference between possible causes and the real cause.** Again, due to time pressures, there is the natural tendency to jump to conclusions that are not based on scientific fact. Under pressure, it can often happen that a possible cause is presumed to be the main cause. The danger lies therein that it may not be. Make sure that you run verification tests to avoid this happening.

9. **Implement permanent corrective measures:** As momentum can wane, especially as time progresses and the pressure has lessened, the most important step can often be overlooked. Make sure that the corrective measures are implemented - and implemented effectively!

10. **Document Results:** Formulate the successes and document them. Consider completing a "Lessons Learned" document for the benefit of others to gain from at a later stage.

11. **Congratulate your Team:** Give credit where credit is due. This motivates! So, with a job well done, don't forget to congratulate your team!

Step D0: Preparing and Planning

This is the first step in the report, called D0. The aim is to complete **a plan of action** or a framework in which the 8D Problem-Solving Process will take place.

Planning your approach will be key to a successful start to the whole 8D process.

Go through the following checklist to see that everything possible is done to ensure this successful start. Start out as you mean to go on!

Checklist for Step 0 of 8D Report

- Have you sufficient knowledge of the 8D process?
- Have you all the details of the complaint or problem?
- Is this complaint registered in the system and has an identification number been allocated to it?
- Have you the details on the problem at hand: identification of the part involved, specification number or part number, quantity, the supplier / the customer in question?
- What are the details of the contact person at the customer or supplier in question? Are there authorities from outside the company to be informed?
- Has top management given the mandate for this process to be carried out?
- Will the team receive sufficient support from the management? Have you a sponsor in management?
- Have you prepared all the initial documents for the process, such as a copy of the 8D report to be used and any training materials needed?

Once the checklist has been passed, fill in the first section of the form:

This is the first section of our form. This template is at the back of the book, or you can download it from our website on our 8D Resources Page. In the following pages, we will be going through each section and each dimension of the 8D report.

DO: Plan	
Set Up Your Plan	
Complaint / Concern / Issue:	
Complaint Reference Number:	
Opened on / Start date:	
Concerned product:	
Customer / Supplier:	
Contact details *(address, Email, contact person, telephone number)* **:**	
Part Number:	

Conclusion:

This section of the 8D report is to set up the planning of your 8D problem-solving activity and to document the exact boundaries of the problem being analyzed.

Noting the start / end times will also help later analysis of all 8D reports and their success as a method of problem-solving within your organization.

Step D1: Form Your Team

In this section of the 8D report, we look at the aspects of **forming your team.**

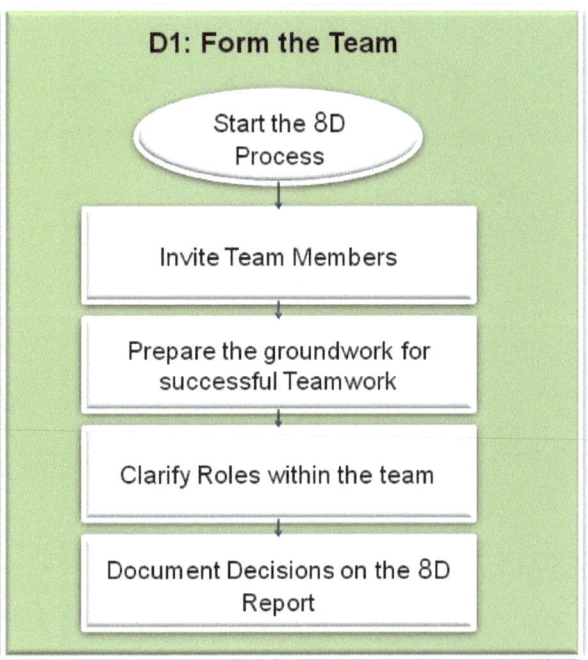

The aim is to form a team with the right people: those with knowledge of the area in question, who are willing, capable and competent to do the task.

- Address the problem with the team.
- Ensure that they are the right people with the proper know-how of any processes or technical areas involved – also of any techniques used.

- Ensure that the team has a champion or a sponsor in management who can support implementation of corrective actions and especially to support decisions when extra resources are needed.
- Ensure a structure in the team with clear responsibilities. Be aware also that the roles can change over time - as the direction of the work may change, the requirements will change also. Make sure the team matches the task at hand.

Go through the following checklist to see that everything possible is done to ensure a successful start.

Checklist for Step 1

- Is your team the right size? (typically 4-10 members).
- Are the appropriate people included (those with the know-how).
- Are the team members clear about the 8D process?
- Are the team roles designated? (sponsor, team leader, moderator, document manager, information-gatherer, someone that ensures that reports get to the right people, someone responsible for any testing that needs to be done, etc.)
- Have you determined who your champion will be?
- Are sufficient resources available? (Meeting rooms, finances, projector, etc.)
- Are the exact targets, including the time-frame, clear to the team?
- Are there confidentiality issues? Are signed confidentiality agreements necessary?
- Are all members clear about the task? (Communicate any limitations, degree of urgency, confidentiality issues, etc.)
- Are reporting priorities clear? (how often reports will be published, who should receive the reports, who should be informed)
- Has the team sufficient support from the management?

Once the Checklist has been passed, fill in Step 1 of the form:

This section of the 8D report is to document the exact details of all members of the team and the champion and the roles they played – even if their roles change over the duration of the process.

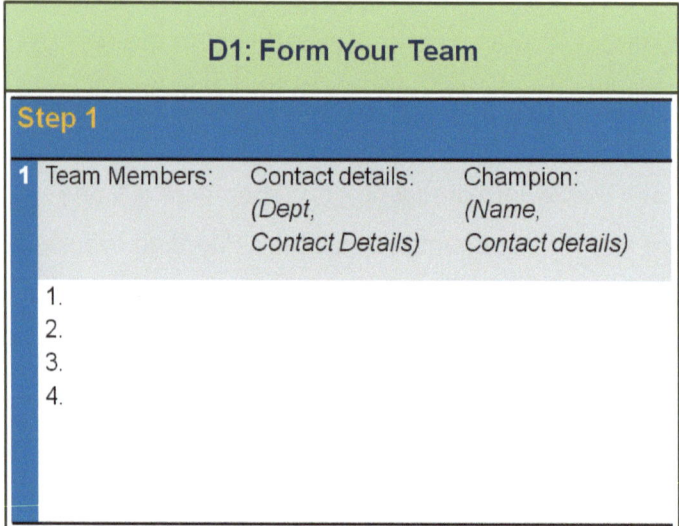

Conclusion:

It is important to document their details so that you know exactly how to contact these people quickly, as well as for follow-up reasons at a later stage. Always remember there can be legal implications to each step in this process.

Should the 8D process not bring the desired results, this can have consequences as the customer may, at most, sue your company or at the very least, move their business elsewhere.

Step D2: Describe the Problem

In this section of the 8d method of problem solving, our aim involves probably the most difficult aspect of the whole 8D Process: **describing the problem**. As Ishikawa said: you will have a problem half solved by defining it correctly on the first day. So this step is really important for a successful outcome.

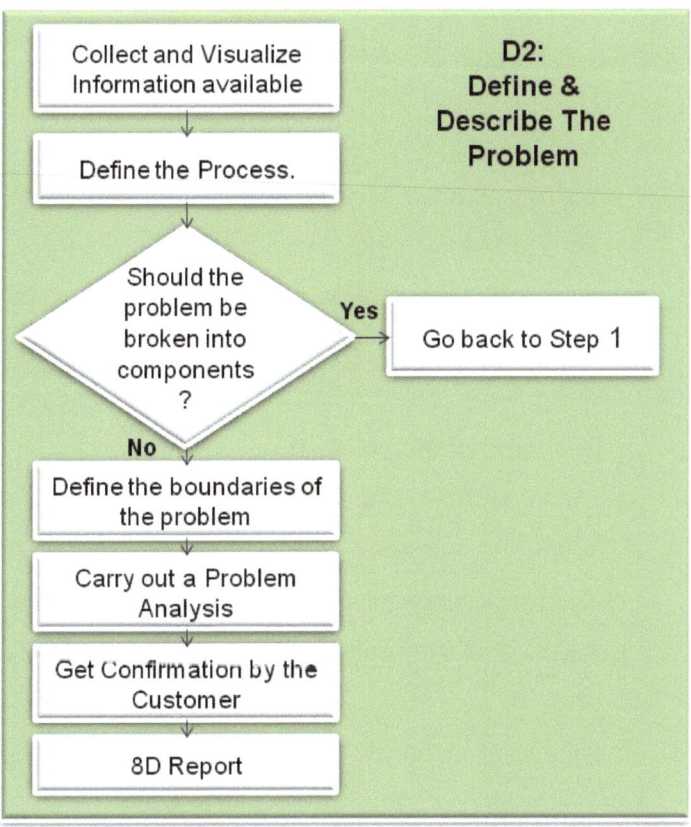

Aim of this step: To clearly and accurately describe the problem.

Outcome: Complete definition of the problem.

Use [problem analysis](#) to define as accurately as possible the problem of the internal or external customer. The internal customer is the receiver of the goods within your company and the external customer is the receiver of your goods that is not within your company.

You can describe your problem using the following three levels:

1. **Symptoms:** Describe what you have observed. How was the problem found? How does the problem appear to you (i.e. the run chart shows a one-sided trend, the machine is making a noise, the customer can't use it because..). This will give you a description of the nature of the problem.
2. **The facts concerning the problem:** What can you or have you measured in relation to the problem. What are the facts concerning this problem? Remember here to look at the problem and not at any potential causes.
3. **The understanding of the problem:** What is your understanding of the problem? This will give the reasoning for the further work you will do in the root cause analysis later in step 4 and any actions you will

decide to take. Consider all aspects of the problem and not only your perspective. Think of the differing ways a software engineer and a mechanic would view the problems in a machine. Try and get an all-encompassing view of the problem. This is also why you need a team of experts involved in the process.

Get to the core of the problem and then, quantify it. Collect as much data and information as possible.

Problem Boundaries

Are the boundaries of the problem clear? This means looking for more information by looking at the what, where, when and the how of the problem. You compare the definition with the inverse possibility.

- If you know **what** the problem is, then be clear about what the problem is not.
- If you know **where** the problem is, ask where isn't this defect or problem occurring? Where being a question of either on the object itself or a question of location.
- If you know **when** this has been a problem, when was it not a problem?
- If you know **how** this is a problem, which aspects are not a problem?

For more on problem statement, boundary examination and relaxation check out our pages:

- Problem Statement
- Boundary Examination
- Boundary Relaxation

Go through the following checklist to see that everything possible is done to ensure that the problem is clearly defined.

Checklist for Step 2

- Is the problem accurately described? (Quality improvement measure, return from customer, safety issues, productivity issues).
- Which customer(s) have been affected?
- Do the authorities need to sign off on this approach?
- Where did the problem occur?
- Are all sources of information on the problem available, and are they clear?
- Was the problem known previously – perhaps in a slightly different manner?
- Is the team constellation still the right one for this task?

8D Problem Solving Process

Once the Checklist has been passed, fill in Step 2 of the form:

This is the section D2 of our form.

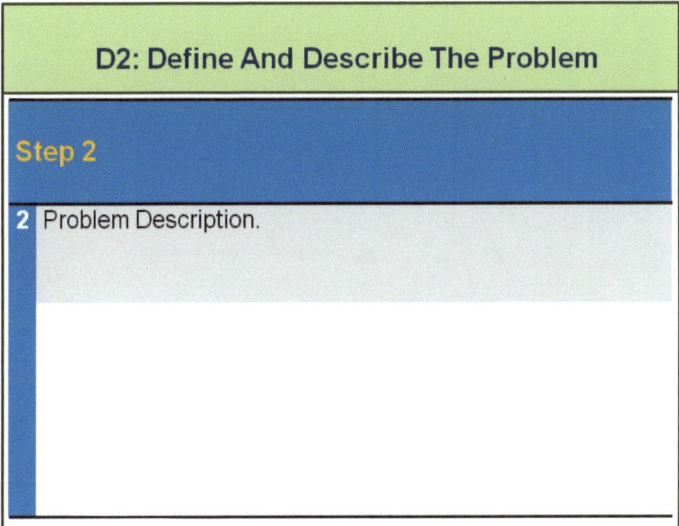

This section Step D2 of the 8D report is to document the problem description. It sets the track for later problem-solving activities.

Note that this stage is focused around getting a really accurate description of the problem. Although very tempting, it should be avoided at all costs to try and jump forward to problem solving without having confirmed the true cause of the problem.

Conclusion:

My advice is not to rush through this stage. Take your time. The better you describe the problem, the closer you will be to finding the root cause. This is not yet the step to look at the root cause! In describing the problem as accurately as you can, you will find often ideas for - as well as the elimination of other- possible root cause(s).

Step D3: Planning Containment Actions

Aim: To protect the customer from the effect of the problem through **containment measures** and to obtain **agreement by the customer** to the measures.

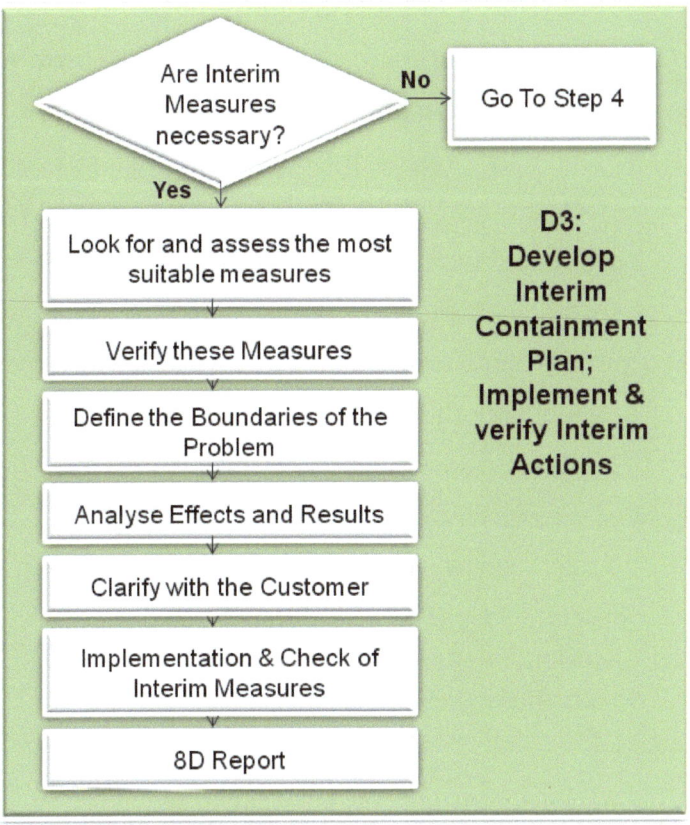

- Organize temporary, interim or containment measures for the control of damage or liability, and check on the effectiveness of these measures.

- Ensure constant checking of the effectiveness of these measures and organize further measures if deemed necessary.
- Be clear about the consequences of the defect or problem. How long can your company live with this problem? The scale of the severity of the problem will define the urgency for action.

Consider setting up a **containment process**, with details on
- how the customer should be assessed as to their situation, their needs and problems as a result f these defective parts;
- how the distribution channels are to be clarified;
- how the containment measures are to be analysed;
- how the containment measures are to be implemented and regularly checked for effectiveness;
- how the responsibilities in these situations are to be laid out, which roles are to be occupied, etc.;
- decision criteria, such as recalling an entire batch when one failure is found, etc.;
- notification rules with details on who is to receive which information, reporting on findings, etc.

Checklist for Step 3

- Are containment measures necessary?
- Are all damaged or failed parts accounted for and the delivery to any other customers prevented?
- Is the best alternative – as a containment measure – chosen after a proper decision analysis?
- Is the choice of containment measures based on facts and figures?
- Do all concerned parties agree with these measures?
- Has the customer agreed to this plan of action?
- Has there been an analysis of potential problems, listing all potential problems, possible causes and preventive measures?
- Has a detailed plan for the introduction of the containment action items been laid out?
- Has the effectiveness of these measures been ensured? How will this effectiveness be checked in order to ensure maintenance of securing the situation?
- Are the containment measures documented and known to all parties involved?
- Is all risk minimized?
- Do you need to inform the customer?

Once the Checklist has been passed, fill in Step 3 of the form:

This is the section D3 of our form.

D3: Develop Interim Containment Plan; Implement and Verify Interim Actions		
Step 3		
3 Immediate Containment Actions.		
Description:	Effect measured:	Date of Implementation:

This section Step D3 of the 8D report is to document the Containment Actions that are undertaken to limit damages done by the problem.

Conclusion

The aim for this step is to take the definition of the problem and decide on measures that will protect your customer.

These containment measures must prevent all damaged or defective parts going to the customer and must therefore receive their approval. They may need to adjust their planning according to the situation. This has the purpose of damage limitation.

As mentioned in many other steps, please be sure to document this section well, as there could be legal implications later on if the damage continues or the risk continues. At the very least, the customer will leave your business with his or her contracts.

The measures taken are meant to be only temporary in nature until a proper resolution is found.

Step D4: Determine the Root Cause

In this section of the 8D Analysis, we look at the steps necessary in completing D4 of the 8D report: **determining the root cause** of the problem.

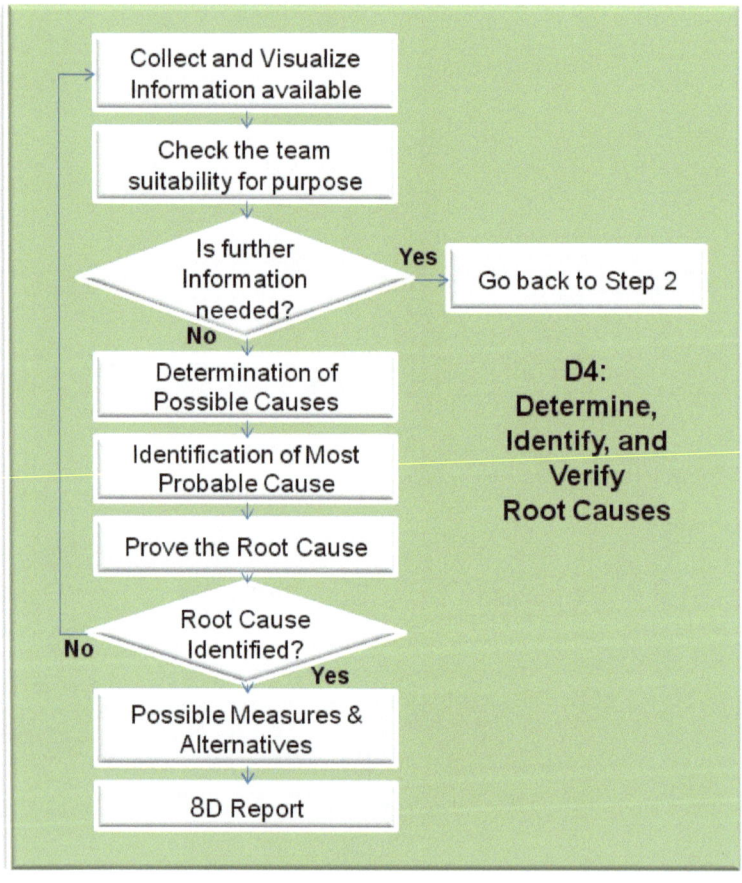

We are now in the phase where we are analyzing the *"Why is this problem here?"* and not the *"What is the*

problem?".

Start out by collecting as much information as possible and making it visual in any way possible. For ways of making your concepts visual, check out these pages on concept mapping.

Analyze using statistical methods and root cause analysis methods such as:

- 5 Whys
- Cause and Effect Diagrams
- Critical to Quality Tree (CTQ)
- Functional Flow Diagram,
- Spray Diagrams,
- Systems Diagram,
- Brainstorming and Affinity Mapping
- Boundary Examination, Boundary Relaxation

If your company is using Design or Product FMEAs (*Failure Mode and Effect Analysis*), use these as a means for evaluating the design or the production processes for root causes to the problem. At the very least the FMEAs must be updated in light of the knowledge gained in this process.

Identify all possible causes that could explain why the problem has occurred. Also identify why the problem was not noticed at the time it occurred. Once the team feels they have found possible root causes, these must be verified by testing them.

Checklist for Step 4

- Is the team still suitable for the task at hand?
- Is a complete assessment or root cause analysis available?
- Are all changes to the process or products completely analyzed?
- Has an analysis of possible causes been carried out?
- Is each possible cause tested to verify that it is a possible cause?
- Is there data on these possible causes so that a quantitative analysis can be carried out?
- Are the possible causes verified?
- Has all documentation been completed?

Once the Checklist has been passed, fill in Step 4 of the form:

This is the section D4 of our form.

8D Problem Solving Process

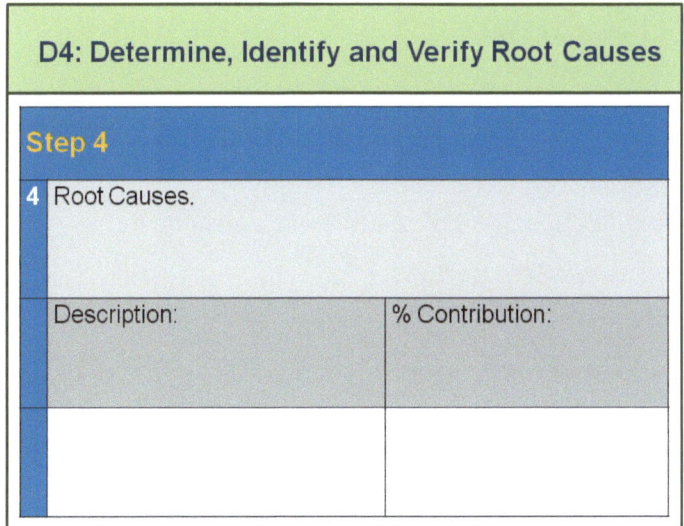

This section Step D4 of the 8D report is to document the work done in analyzing the root cause(s) of the problem. Add all further documentation of root cause analyses to the report, each item must be clearly identified.

Conclusion:

This section of the 8D report is to document the exact details of all root causes as determined by the team. It is important to give an indication of the probable contribution of the named causes to the problem. This way, priorities can be made, especially if financial resources are needed to solve the problem.

Step D5: Choosing & Verifying Corrective Actions

The 8D Step D5 has the aim of **choosing and verifying permanent corrective actions**.

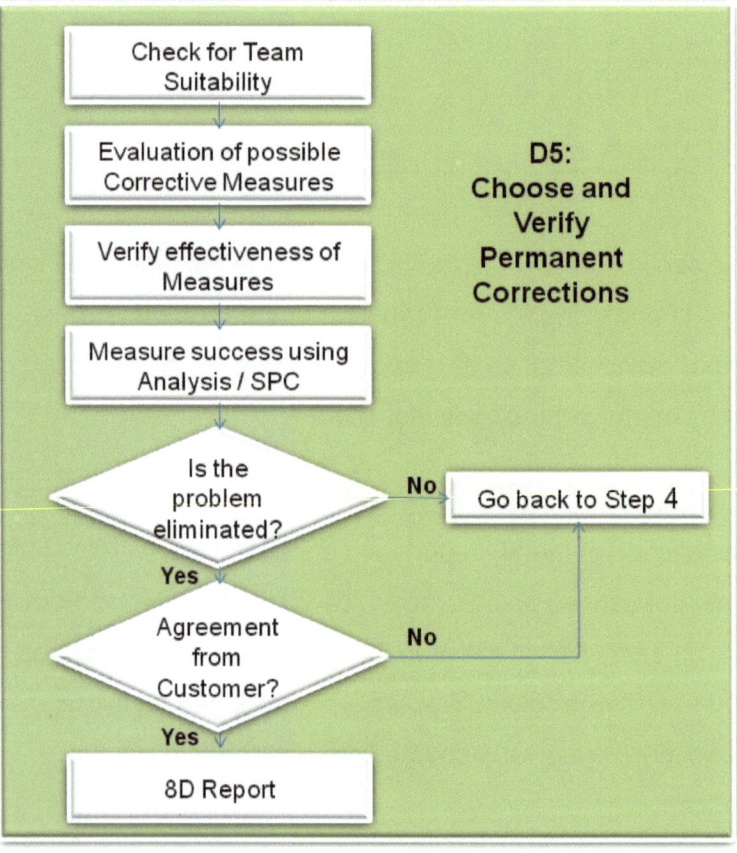

Through pre-production tests, quantitatively confirm that the selected correction will resolve the problem for the customer. (Verify that the correction will actually solve the problem.)

Checklist for Step 5

- Is your team still suitable for the job at hand, or is further expertise required?
- Are the corrective measures that are to be carried out, defined correctly? (who, what, where, when and how)
- Has a decision analysis been carried out?
- Have the corrective measures been assessed?
- Were alternatives to the measures chosen taken into consideration?
- Has a risk analysis of these measures been carried out?
- Is there a plan detailing the steps necessary to introduce these measures?
- Is appropriate monitoring set up or planned?
- Has an FMEA been carried out? Or existing FMEAs updated?
- Is there evidence that these measures are effective? In particular, have field tests or production tests been carried out?
- Has the customer been informed?
- Is the documentation for this step complete?

Once the Checklist has been passed, fill in Step 5 of the form:

D5: Determine, Identify & Verify Corrective Actions			
Step 5			
5	Long-term Corrective Actions.		
	Description:	Verification of Effectiveness:	Carried out by:

This section of the 8D report is to document the exact details of all corrective actions.

Conclusion

It is really important that the identified action that will eliminate the cause of the problem is verified. Will this problem really disappear and re-occur if you remove the cause and re-introduce the cause? If not, then this was not the root cause but simply a contributor and you may have to go back to step D4.

In some cases, you may not be able to identify one single root cause but can identify a number if contributors.

The key is in the title of this step.

Choosing: List up the potential choices, then, decide on which ones to implement.

Corrective: Ensure the measures are "correcting" the problem.

Actions: Ensure the actions are actually carried out!

Verifying: Go back and check - is the problem really gone?

Step D6: Set Corrective Measures

This is the Step D6: **Implement and Validate Corrective Actions**: Define and Implement the best corrective actions.

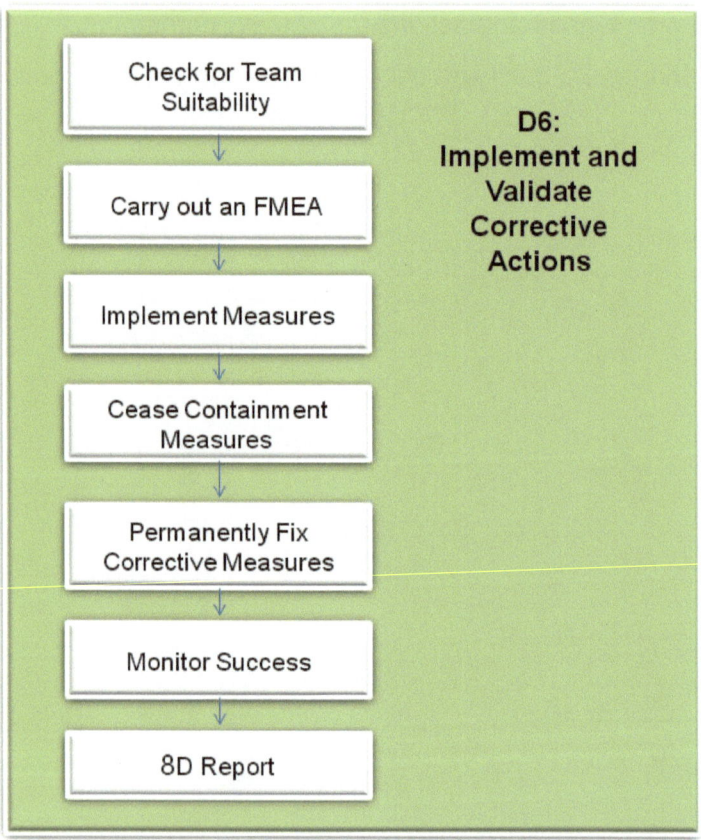

Go through the following checklist to see that everything possible is done to ensure this step is successful.

Review the FMEAs: reassess the severity, occurrence and the new control levels for these items in the FMEA report.

Validation Tools

Validate these initiatives using tools such as:
- Variance Analysis
- SPC Analysis, i.e. correlation factors and similar
- Balanced Scorecard, if used.
- Follow up on the Critical-to-Quality Drivers
- Update your Measurement System Analysis

Cost of Quality Analysis

Now that the containment actions can be ceased, carry out a cost of quality analysis. This is where you assess how much the containment action(s) cost together with the loss at the customer against the investment for corrective action.

Documentation

At this stage, all documentation must be together and each item clearly identified and linked to the central document, the 8D report. The documents must include:
- all correspondence concerning the 8D process steps so far, especially all correspondence with the customer and where applicable, external authorities.
- Documentation of all decisions made.
- Documentation of all tests carried out with the reports on the results.

The aim is to have all documentation filed and archived in such a way that follow-up at a later date, for whatever reason, is easily possible.

Checklist for Step 6

- Are the measures clearly defined and up to standard? Are they validated?
- Has the customer given a positive assessment of the results from introducing these measures?
- Have the necessary changes to the process been carried out?
- Has the effectiveness of the monitoring been tested?
- Is the agreement by all affected parties available for the introduction of these measures? This must include external authorities that should be informed.
- Are emergency measures determined in case the original measures cannot be implemented?
- Is the documentation for this step complete?
- Has the FMEA been updated?
- Check if there is any remaining risk and whether this should be signed off by top management.

Once the Checklist has been passed, fill in Step 6 of the form:

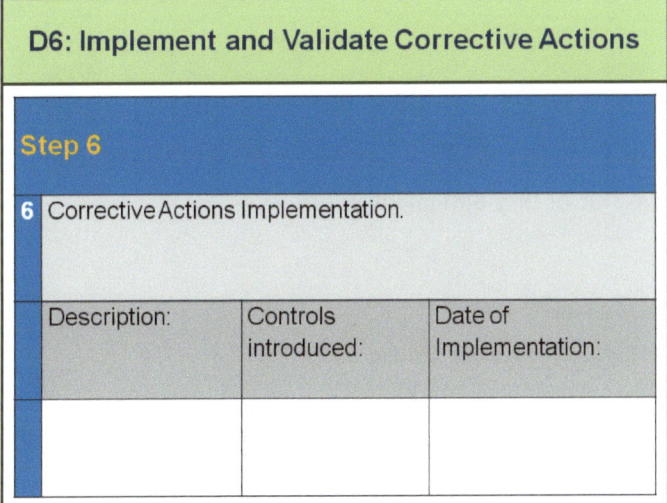

This section of the 8D report is to document the exact details of the implementation and validation of all corrective actions.

Conclusion:

This section of the 8D report is to document the exact details of all corrective actions that have been implemented: the type of corrective action, how they will be managed or controlled and the dates of implementation.

It is important to have your documentation in order. All details are to be documented, so that you know exactly what the corrective actions are and there is a clear follow-through how decisions were met. This is important for further use within your company as well as for the obvious legal reasons. The aim is to have all risks to your company avoided completely or in the worst case, reduced to an absolute minimum..

Step D7: Take Preventive Measures

This is section D7: **Taking Preventive Measures.** The aim of this section is to prevent the original problem ever occurring again - that or any similar problem.

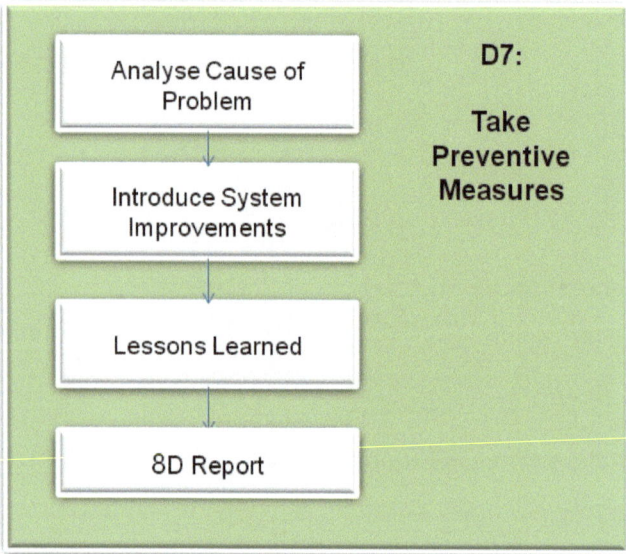

This step is about taking a 360 degree look around to see if there could be a similar risk in the company for generating the same problem. If a new production line is to be set up with the knowledge gained after this case, will it be done in the same way as before or can the knowledge be used to improve that design?

The important message is to implement the **lessons learned** here in order to make the new designs more sustainable and get maximum value out of the work done in the 8D process.

At a very minimum, use the knowledge gained here to develop your containment action process further so that you can make the effect of such problems occurring in the future less severe.

This part of the process takes you through these steps:

- Check the trigger of the problem or what triggered the whole situation. Has that been dealt with? Would it possibly trigger off some sort of similar problem?
- Now that all possible recurrence has been avoided, the next step is to update the system or systematic approach that takes place around where the root cause was. This means, for example, updating procedures, retraining employees, putting new measuring equipment in place, changing checking procedures, etc.
- Once the whole corrective action has been clarified and implemented, check for opportunities to replicate these corrections within the company. Are there other processes which would benefit from the same improvements?
- Then finally, obviously not a "must" but a well recommended step to take to get maximum value out of all work done here in the 8D steps: document the lessons that were learnt along the way. At some stage, hopefully later rather than sooner, the knowledge gained in doing

the 8D will be extremely valuable in some other situation. Particularly in view of the trends towards frequent job changes of employees, this would be one way to retain the knowledge within the organization.

8D Problem Solving Process

Checklist for Step 7

- Are the reasons for the problem occurring now fully clarified?
- Are the influencing factors fully clear?
- Have all changes to the system or the organization been carried out?
- Has this implemented measure been included in the appropriate documentation –process documentation, test specifications, etc. – and are the employees informed?
- Has an FMEA been carried out? (For 2nd or 3rd tier suppliers to the automobile industry)

Once the Checklist has been passed, fill in Step 7 of the form:

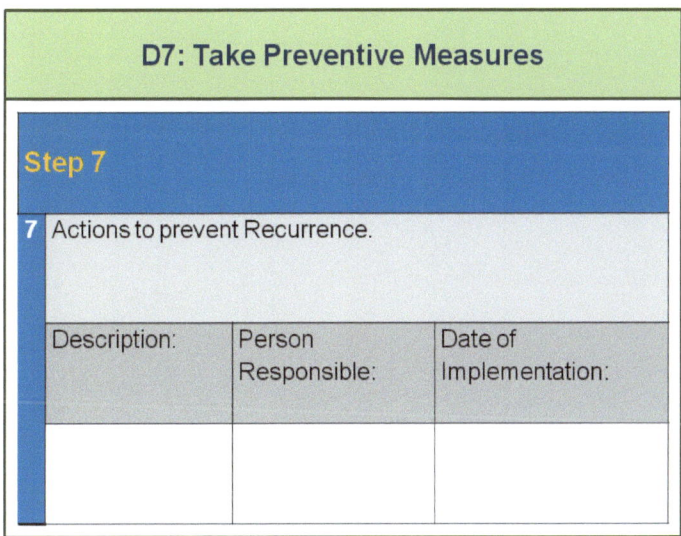

This section of the 8D report focuses on documenting the exact details of all preventive measures and 8D steps for D7.

Conclusion:

As with all other sections, the documentation of these details will potentially have legal implications, so it is important to keep all documentation cleanly filed and traceable.

Consider at this stage the 360 degree view: the complete look around for implications or effects on other processes within your company, including other sites, other customers, other products, future designs, future production lines, etc.

This is the stage where the benefits can be harvested out of the work done. By replicating the improvements in other processes, by documenting the knowledge gained for later use, by avoiding these problems occurring elsewhere, you are maximizing the cost investments placed in this 8D process.

Check, have you just *"spent a dollar to save a dime"*? Was this 8D Cost beneficial or cost-intensive?

Step 8: Congratulate Your Team

The final step in the 8D process is to **congratulate your team**.

This step has the three steps of

Finalising the documentation

See step 6 for details on what is expected with the documentation. This includes gathering all the documentation in a file together and archiving it in a traceable and retrievable manner.

You should also add to the documentation the viewpoint of the customer. How was the impact of this problem for the customer? –Both the initial impact with cost implications and then later, the impact of the work that was done. What was the impact on sales and on the relationship with the customer? Has the relationship with this customer benefitted from the work done?

Give feedback to the team members.

Please give feedback to each and every team member. Evaluate and verify the 8D process itself: what has been learned from this methodology, learning about the process after carrying it through. Consider how the participants could perform better in a team. If conflict arose during the process, make sure that this conflict has been sorted out. Have the team members congratulated each other and shown their appreciation of the efforts made?

We advise to celebrate what would have gone wrong but didn't because of the work done by the team. The cost of the celebration should be in relation to the effort of the team and the impact on business and the customer.

Give great recognition where great recognition is warranted. While typically, the majority of people who are involved in such a process consider it to be "part of the job", review if the work done could be linked to the individual's performance appraisal.

Recognition by the management:

The management and you must congratulate your team. One of the most important steps is that management play their role in recognizing and showing their appreciation for the work done.

Consider making some of the findings public, especially how you have maximized the benefit from all the work done.

Some Ideas on how to congratulate your team:

- Award all those involved with a certificate or pens: give an acknowledgement of their achievement.
- Make up team plaques, trophies, certificates, mugs, pens, T-shirts, etc.
- Carry out a special treat.
- Publicize photos, charts or posters showing the team's achievement.
- Have the team featured on company website or in the business newsletter.
- Have a senior manager call by the team to express a special thanks or make a presentation.
- Enable the teams to do a make-over of their working environment.
- Support the team set up a presentation of their work to others, with a booth, display case, photos, etc.
- Have the team present their accomplishments to executives, visitors, organizational meetings, etc.
- Carry out a team trip to external partners.

Celebrate your successes!

Checklist for Step 8

- Is all the documentation complete and in a presentable, understandable fashion stored in a retrievable place – in paper form or digitally?
- Are all possible after-effects of any tension or conflict within the team solved?
- Have the individual team members congratulated each other?
- Has the performance of each team member been recognized by top management?
- Has there been a celebration?

Once the Checklist has been passed, fill in Step 8 of the form:

D8: Congratulate Your Team		
Step 8		
8 Congratulate Your Team	Report Closing Date:	Produced By: *(Contact details)*

Conclusion

This is the final and closing section of the report. The main points in this section are to

1. Document carefully for potential users at a later stage
2. Ensure recognition within and of the team of the effort that has gone into the work done. This is also extremely important for others watching who will be asked at a later stage to take part in a similar process.

As with all other sections, the documentation of these details may have legal implications, so it is important to keep that always in mind.

We wish you every success in your work!

Best Wishes,

Martha & the Business Online Learning Team!

8D Report Template

This template is available for download on our page 8D Resources.

DISCLAIMER: *The following sample only serves as an example for the answers to the questions for an 8D Process. All information below is fabricated and not real. The following answers should ONLY be considered as idea generator for answering the questions. Nothing in the answers implies that it would be considered as the best solutions.*

Complaint / Concern / Issue	100 Pieces of Part Number G11B5 were returned due to oxidation on the surface.
Complaint Reference Number:	CC2013/05/A42
Opened on / Start date:	16.June.2013
Concerned product:	Die Cast Parts G11B5
Customer / Supplier:	Sample Supplier Ltd.
Contact details (address, Email, contact person, telephone number):	Mr Angry Customer, 091-55575, angry.customer@sample-supplier.com
Part Number:	G11B5

Step 1

Team Members:	Contact details: *(Dept, Email, etc.)*	Champion: *(Name, Contact details)*
1. John Smyth	John.Symth@Ourfirm.com	Ms. Angela Fields
2. Mary Black	Mary.black@ourfirm.com	Quality Manager
3. Harry White	Harry.white@ourfirm.com	Our Firm Ltd.
4. Sally Trunk	Sally.trunk@ourfirm.com	Angela.fields@ourfirm.com
5. Mark Hall (as from Step6)	Mark.hall@ourfirm.com	

Step 2

2. Problem Description.

100 die-cast parts were returned from Sample Supplier on 10.06.2013.
The parts were from Batch Number 68514A. Manufacturing Date: 31.05.13.
Total Batch amount: 350. Delivery to customer: 07.05.13. Passed our final Inspection date:06.05.2013.
Returned Parts Check Results:
The parts were oxidised far beyond the acceptable level. Surface Roughness Out of Tolerance.
Parts Packaging on return to company checked: Okay.

Step 3

3. Immediate Containment Actions.

Description:	Effect measured:	Date of Implementation:
Stocks checked 50 pcs. in stores. Placed in quarantine.	All parts successfully located and prevented from future use.	16.06.2013
100 pcs in transport to customer. Stopped and request for return placed.	Under observation until further notice.	16.06.2013
100% Inspection at Outgoing Quality.	Employees sensitized to problem	16.06.2013
Parts given to Diecasting for testing.		

Step 4

4. Root Causes.

Description:	% Contribution:
After thorough Investigation and analysis the following were found to be the root causes to the problem:	Methods Used: Cause and effect Analysis, 5 Whys, Functional Flow Diagram.
1. Insufficient Visual Inspection Training for new employees in Outgoing Quality.	30%
2. Insufficient Quality Inspection in Die-casting area.	30%
3. Chemical Anti-oxidising agent ineffective.	40%

Step 5

5. Long-term Corrective Actions.

Description:	Verification of Effectiveness:	Carried out by:
1. HR Training procedures newly defined with immediate Implementation.	1. Taken up in internal audit programme	Internal Auditors in Q-Dept. HR Reporting to Top Management, quoting also results of internal audits.
2. Chemical Anti-oxidising Agent audited by our Vendor Engineer and Diecasting engineer.	2. Monthly progress reporting to management until further notice. Audit results to be presented to Top Management for further details.	Mr. John Smyth Ms. Sally Trunk

8D Problem Solving Process

Step 6

6. Corrective Actions Implementation.

Description:	Controls introduced:	Date of Implementation:
1. Outgoing Visual Training updated. All employees re-trained.	Mary Black John Smyth Sally Trunk	01.07.2013 25.06.2013 10.07.2013
2. Diecasting employees retrained in testing.	Mark Hall Sally Trunk	20.06.2013
3. New testing methods introduced to test Chemical Antioxidant by incoming.		
4. Incoming tests set to high level testing.		

Step 7

7. Actions to prevent Recurrence.

Description:	Person Responsible:	Date of Implementation:
1. Internal audit will take up internal testing as a priority.	Mark Hall Sam Junt, Purchasing	17.06.2013 14.07.2013
2. Second source for Supplier sourced, tested and approved.		

Step 8

8. Congratulate your Team

	Report Closing Date:	Produced by: *(Contact details)*
Team congratulated by top management with special meal. Photos to be seen on Company Website.	14.07.2013	John Smyth

About the Author

Martha Begley Schade holds a B.Sc. in Physics and Maths from the National University of Galway, Ireland, and a Masters Degree in Business Administration.

Martha has over 27 years' management and consultancy experience in the Quality and Production areas in Ireland, Germany and around Europe.

She has designed and developed Global Management Systems for Purchasing, Quality, Human Resources, E-learning, Self Assessment training and provided trainings on these topics, worldwide.

Martha is an approved Auditor and Assessor for the ISO9000 standards as well as the EFQM Awards. She also has a Green Belt in Six Sigma.

In 2011, she launched http://www.business-online-learning.com, a free resource for adult learners and those who wish to upgrade their employability..

We invite you to join us:

www.ingramcontent.com/pod-product-compliance
Lightning Source LLC
Chambersburg PA
CBHW041107180526

45172CB00001B/151